Welcome to ScratchJr!

In this book you'll learn how to use the reco[rd] free ScratchJr app to record your own voice effects. You'll find out how to add your sound effects to your interactive stories, create a band and use sound to make useful apps for everyday living.

Find out more at go.techagekids.com

Let's get coding!

Elbrie & Tracy

TECH AGE™ KIDS

Whatever device you use for the projects, make sure you allow the ScratchJr app access to your microphone and camera.

Bubble pop

ScratchJr comes with a pop sound. Let's make a bubble pop when you tap it.

This is the **home** icon. Tap here to find your **projects** and start new ones.

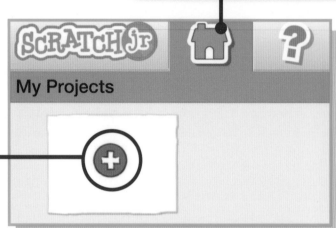

My Projects

① Open ScratchJr by tapping the **app logo**. Then start a **new project** by tapping here.

② To create a **new character** tap this icon, then the **paintbrush**.

③ Tap a **colour** then the **circle tool** and make a circle with your finger.

④ Tap the **fill tool** to fill the circle with colour.

Don't worry if you make a mistake, you can **undo** a step by tapping this **arrow**.

To make the circle look like a bubble, draw a thin curved line using the **line tool** and white colour to add a bit of shine.

Line tool

Circle tool

Bubble

Objects are called **characters** too.

Fill tool

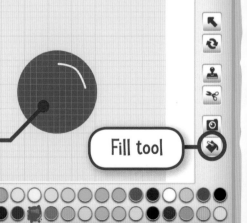

⑤ Tap the **tick** to save.

(6) Use your **finger** to drag the bubble to the side of the kitten.

(7) Tap on the **yellow coding block**. Can you see this block?

This is a **start on tap block**. The code will only run when you tap the character on the stage.

Tap this **reset** icon to return characters to their **start positions**.

Coding blocks

Coding area

(8) Drag the **start on tap block**, into the bubble's **coding area** with your finger.

(9) Tap on the other coloured **coding blocks**. Find these blocks, drag them to the **coding area** and join them up.

Bubble code

This code uses the green **sound block** and a purple **hide block**. It tells the bubble to **pop** and **hide** (disappear) when you tap it.

(10) Tap the bubble to see what happens, then tap the **reset** icon at the top of the page to **start the code** again.

What colour are the **sound blocks** in Scratch Jr? Tick the correct colour.

red   green   blue

Try adding another bubble in a different colour. Can you get that bubble to pop too?

ANSWERS: Sound blocks are green

Well done!

Say "hello"

Record your own voice for a character so they can say "hello" to the ScratchJr kitten.

Oh, hello!

① Start a **new project** and add a **new character**. Choose one of the children.

② Tap on the green **sound block** and then tap on the **microphone block**.

You may get a message asking **permission** to access the microphone on your device. Tap 'yes'!

While you're **talking**, some of the bars will light up green. The louder you talk the more bars light up.

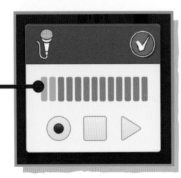

③ A box will pop up with a **screen recorder**. Tap the red **circle** to begin recording.

④ Say "hello" and then press the **square** to finish recording.

⑤ Press the **triangle** to play your recording, then tap the **tick**. If you're not happy with it, **record** again.

Circle the **code block** you should tap to record a sound or your voice.

ANSWER: The green block with the microphone is the recording sound block

(6) Find these blocks and drag them into the child's **coding area**.

Child code

This code tells the recording to **play** when the character is **tapped**.

The new sound block will appear in the green **sound section**. Each sound belongs to **one character**. You can't share sounds between characters.

(7) Add a **background** by tapping this icon. Scroll through to find this **empty room scene** and tap the **tick**.

(8) Using your finger **move** the kitten and child so they're next to each other.

(9) Tap on the kitten and use steps 2 to 5 to **record** a message, then drag these **coding blocks** into the kitten's coding area.

Don't forget to tap the **characters** to try out your project.

Try adding another **character**. What would you like them to say? Write it here.

Ask someone else to record their voice and say something silly!

Well done!

Creating sounds

ScratchJr has lots of different characters and you can create sounds and funny voices for them all.

① Start a **new project** and choose one of the creatures below as a **new character**.

How do you think these creatures might sound - happy, noisy, silly? Write your ideas next to each creature.

② Tap the **paintbrush** on the character to change its **name**.

Tap the **name space** to type in a name.

Tac

③ Record the **sound** for your creature by tapping on its **microphone block**.

All ScratchJr **projects** start with this kitten character. If you don't need it, tap and hold the character until you see an **X**. Tap the **X** to delete the kitten.

④ Add this **code** to your creature, so it makes the **sound effect** when you tap on it.

If you make a **mistake** placing a code, tap this back arrow.

⑤ Add the other creatures as **new characters** and record their **sounds**.

⑥ Add the **same code** as step 4 to each creature and add a **background**.

Each **sound** belongs to one character. You can't **share** sounds between characters.

⑦ Tap the **full-screen icon** to test your project. Tap each creature to hear their **sounds**.

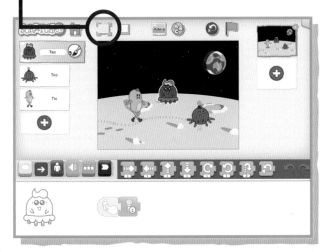

⑧ Tap the **full-screen icon** again if you want to amend your project.

Try this challenge, then tick the box when you've completed it.

I can make my creatures say "hello" to each other in funny voices.

Hello!

Well done!

Record a play

In this project you're going to create a play with two people talking to each other.

Don't forget to delete the kitten. See p9 for how to do this.

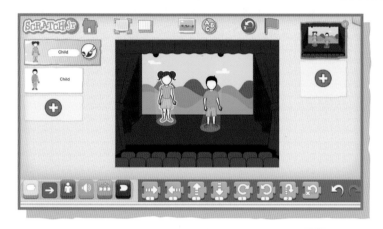

① Begin a **new project** with the theatre **background** and choose two people.

② Now, fill in the **missing words** in the play script.

Character 1: Hello, my name is

Character 2: Hi. I'm

Character 1: I've just found a

Character 2: Wow! Can you show me?

③ Tap the first character and the **microphone sound block**. Record the first line of the play to create a **recorded sound block** with a number 1 on it.

④ Tap on the **other character** and record this character's first line. This will create a **sound block** with number 1 for this character.

Be careful to record the correct lines for each character!

(5) Record the second line for Character 1, which will create another **sound block** (this one will have a number 2 on it).

(6) Record the second line for Character 2 in the same way, then add the **code blocks** below to each character.

Character 1 code

This code uses a **green flag** as a starting block. The character will speak then send a **message** to Character 2.

Character 2 code

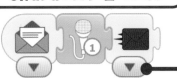

This code starts when Character 2 receives the orange **message block**. It will speak, then send a red **message block** to Character 1.

> Tap on the **down arrow** of this coding block to change the envelope to red.

(7) Now, add these **separate parts** of code alongside the first parts of code for each character.

Extra Character 1 code

When Character 1 receives the red **message block** it will start to speak. Then it will send a blue **message block** to Character 2.

Extra Character 2 code

When Character 2 receives the blue **message block** it will start to speak the last line of the play.

(8) Tap the **green flag** at the top of your screen to **start** your project.

Tick the boxes when you've:

☐ re-recorded a bit of the speech

☐ changed the colour of a message block

☐ made Character 2 speak at the right time

Well done!

Rhythm rounds

It's time to make some music! Code each character to make a different sound and create rhythms with your code.

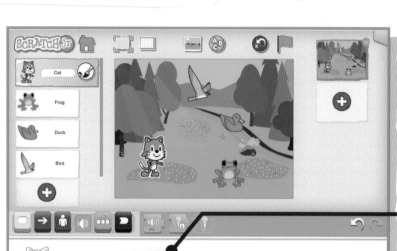

① Start a **new project** and add four **new characters**.

② Add a **new background** of your choice.

③ Record a sound for each character, then add **code** like this so it plays when you **tap** it.

Here are some ideas for **recording** sounds:

clap your hands

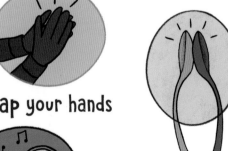

tap spoons together

stamp your foot

sing like a bird (or record a real one)

press a doorbell

Try tapping on the characters at different times to see what happens.

Write some of your own sound ideas here.

④ Use the **code** below to create a **longer sequence** with a **repeat block** and **wait block** with the sound you created.

⑤ Create a background **rhythm** by recording a new sound. Use a **green flag** start block.

Longer sequence code

Rhythm code

These codes use an orange **wait block** to add a pause. You can change the **length of time** to wait by tapping on the number and using the **keypad** to change the number. The **repeat block** repeats that section of code, and the **forever** block tells the code to keep repeating.

⑥ Now you've got a background **rhythm** and a **longer sequence** of sound, tap the **green flag** to start.

⑦ Keep **tapping** the characters to add their **sounds** to the mix. Tweak the code until you're happy!

Circle which of these **coding blocks** can be used to trigger the sounds to **start**.

Use the red hexagon at the top of your screen to stop your code from running if you've used a **repeat forever** block.

ANSWERS: All of these can be used to start your code except the red hexagon

Well done!

13

Talking story

You can create talking stories with ScratchJr.
The characters in this story are two dogs!

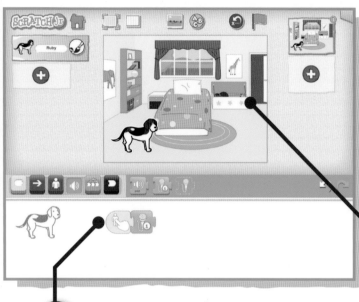

① Start a **new project** and find this bedroom **background**.

② Add a dog as a **new character**, and name it Ruby. Drag Ruby to the floor.

Turn back to p8 to remind yourself how to name characters.

③ **Record** Ruby saying, "Hi, I'm Ruby." Add the **start on tap** block and your recorded **sound block** to Ruby's coding area.

④ Add a **ball character and** drag it to the top of the toy box.

⑤ Using the boxes below, plan the **code** to get the ball to bounce, then add the code to the ball's **coding area**.

How high would you like the ball to bounce and how many times? Write the numbers here.

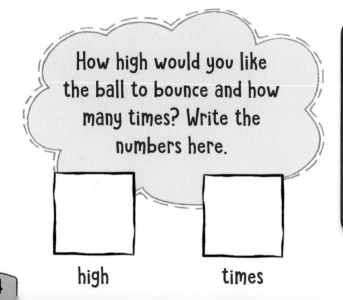

high   times

Ball code

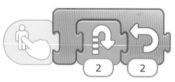

This code tells the ball to **bounce** twice when you tap it. You can tap the number on the bottom of the coding blocks, then use the pop-up **keypad** to change the number of bounces.

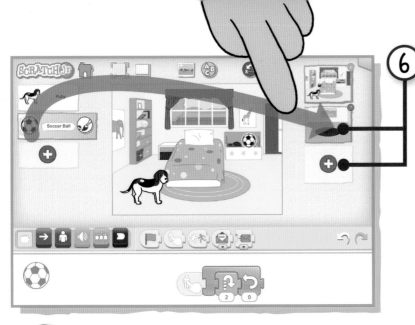

⑥ Tap here to add a **new page** and choose this empty room **background**.

Each new page needs its own characters, so remember to add them each time.

⑦ Tap back on to the **first page** and **drag** the ball from the **left-hand panel** over onto the **second page**. The ball and all its code will now appear on the **second page**.

⑧ Add Ruby again and **record** her saying, "I'm a bit bored. Where shall I go?"

⑨ Add a **start on tap block** and this sound block to Ruby's coding area. Tap the **full-screen icon** to test your story so far.

⑩ Use these **arrows** to move through the pages. **Tap** the characters to make them **speak** and move.

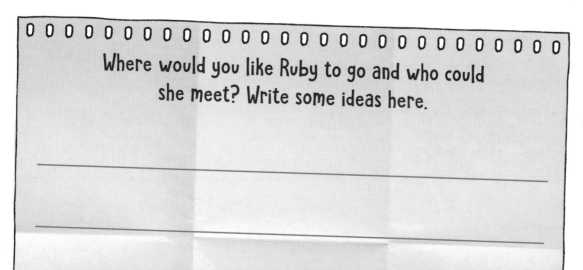

Where would you like Ruby to go and who could she meet? Write some ideas here.

Can Ruby come and play with me?

Continued...

11 Add a **third page** and find this suburbs **background**.

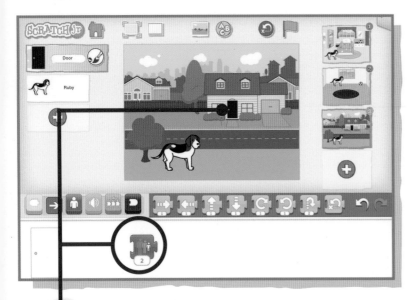

12 Create a **new character** and tap the **paintbrush**. Draw a door then tap the **tick**.

> Turn back to p4 if you've forgotten how to draw a new character.

13 Drag a purple **shrink block** into the door's **coding area**. Tap it to make the door **small** enough to sit on top of the other door in the scene. **Drag** your door into position.

14 Record a doorbell **sound effect**, then add this code to the door's coding area.

Door code

This code will play your doorbell **sound** then make the door **wiggle** a bit when you tap it!

15 Add Ruby and the ball to this **third page**. (Remember you can drag Ruby and the ball from a previous page.)

Can you tick which **blue** motion block you could use to make Ruby walk forwards?

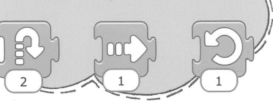

16 Record Ruby saying, "Hello friend! Can you come and play?" Add the **start on tap** block and your recorded **sound block** to Ruby's coding area.

ANSWER: The motion block in the middle will move Ruby forwards

(17) Add a **fourth page** and find the park **background**.

(18) Add Ruby, the ball and another dog **character**. Tap on the **paintbrush** to change this dog's **colour** and give it a name.

What could the dogs **say** to each other? Write it here, then **record** and code the dogs.

_____

_____

_____

_____

_____

(19) Try using some of the **blue motion blocks** to make Ruby and her friend **move** around.

Don't forget you can change the **number** of steps a character moves by **tapping** on the number on the **motion block**.

When you test the code for movement, tap this **reset** icon if you want to get a character back to the **start position**.

Why not try to add more characters in the park that **move** and make sounds.

(20) Tap **full-screen mode** and use the **arrows** at the bottom to test your project.

Well done!

Record your own story

Here's where you can plan, create and record your own story.

Remember that objects in ScratchJr are also called characters.

① Choose your **characters** and introduce them, then decide **where** your story will **begin**.

② Fill in the plan below for your **first page**.

What kind of scene will you use as a background?	Who will your characters be?

What sound effects will you use?	What will your characters do or say?

③ You can either create the **first page** now or plan the **whole story** first. Look back at Ruby's story if you need help.

You don't have to have all of your characters on the first page, you can introduce more later.

④ Think about what **coding blocks** you want to use. Look back over the pages to remind yourself.

Tick the boxes when you've:

☐ used a **start on tap** block

☐ recorded two **sound effects**

☐ recorded **speech** for a character

⑤ Add a **second page**. This is where you introduce a **problem** for your characters. In Ruby's story, the problem was that Ruby was feeling bored.

What kind of scene will you use as a background?

The problem is...

Which new characters will you need?

What will your characters do or say?

What sound effects will you use?

You can only have **four pages** for each project.

Continued...

(6) Add a **third page**. This is where the **problem** starts to get fixed and is called the **resolution**.

Remember, you can **draw** your own characters by tapping on the **paintbrush**.

What kind of scene will you use as a background?

What will your characters do or say?

Which characters are needed for this part of the story?

The beginning of the resolution is...

What sound effects will you use?

You can record **real sounds** to add to your story. Try recording birds, the washing machine or a ticking clock.

(7) Keep **checking** your project as you go — use the **full-screen mode** then this **reset icon**.

8 The **fourth page** is the last page of your project and the end of your story.

Try changing your voice for different characters or recording a friend or sibling.

What kind of scene will you use as a background?

What will your characters do or say?

Which characters are needed for this part of the story?

What sound effects will you use?

The end of the resolution is...

9 When all your pages are finished, check your **code** and fix any **bugs** (mistakes in the program). Then you can view your project in **full-screen** and show it to your friends and family!

Well done!

Sing a song

Try this project to create code for a longer recording of a song or rhyme.

① Think of a song or rhyme you know well. Start a **new project** with a **background** that fits with your song.

② Add two **new characters** to sing the song.

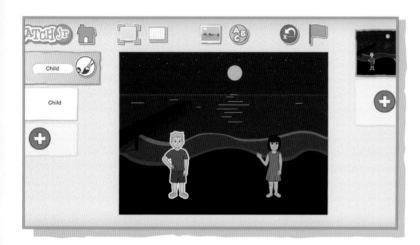

We've chosen 'Twinkle, Twinkle Little Star', but you can choose a **song** or **rhyme** you like or make one up yourself.

Twinkle, twinkle, little star,
How I wonder what you are!
Up above the world so high,
Like a diamond in the sky.

③ Write **down** the words to your song here and work out which of your **characters** will sing which part of your song.

You could even write a **new song** about me!

4 **Record** your song with the different **characters** singing different **parts**. (You could even try to code a **different page** for each line or verse.)

Remember you can have four pages for each project.

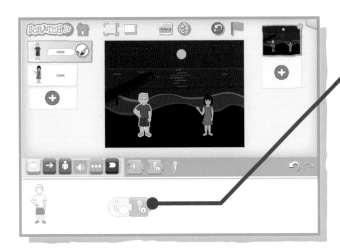

5 Add this **code** to each of your characters, so the song plays when you **tap** them.

Remember to use the correct **sound block** in each character's code, so they sing the correct lines!

6 Add **new characters** to help **animate** (bring to life) parts of the song. We've added a **star** and coded it to spin.

7 Use the **blue motion blocks** and try coding your characters to **move** while they sing.

Star code

This code tells the star to **grow**, **shrink** then **rotate** and to **repeat forever**.

8 Use the **full-screen mode** to test your project.

Tick the boxes when you've:

☐ sung part of the song in a silly voice

☐ coded a character to walk around

☐ explored using different start blocks

Well done!

Creature quiz

This project will help you plan a quiz app to test your knowledge about different animals.

① Add the jungle **background** to a **new** project. Add the bird, butterfly, monkey and lizard **characters**.

② **Drag** them apart so they're in different areas of the jungle.

③ Add the mushroom **character**, place it near the other mushrooms and add this code.

Mushroom code

This code tells a **speech bubble** to pop up from the mushroom when the **green flag** is tapped.

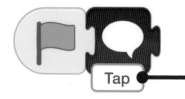

④ Tap the text on this code block. Type "Tap me!" into the **speech bubble** text.

⑤ **Record** this speech for the mushroom character: "Can you tap on the mammal in this picture?"

Which creature is the **mammal** in your picture? Write the **answer** here.

⑥ Now add this extra **code**.

Extra mushroom code

This code tells the **recording** to play when you **tap** the mushroom.

(7) Each of the creatures needs to give an answer when it's tapped, so **record** a message for each **character**. Here's what they could say:

Bird: "Not me, I'm a bird".
Butterfly: "Not me, I'm an insect."
Monkey: "That's right! I'm a mammal."
Lizard: "Not me, I'm a reptile."

What type of creature am I?

Write down your own ideas here.

_____

_____

_____

_____

(8) Record the **speech** for each animal then add the **code** below to each creature.

Animal code

This code tells the animal to **speak** when you **tap** it, then **hide**.

You might not want to use the **hide block** for the monkey. Perhaps the monkey could **jump** or **spin** instead?

(9) Test your quiz in **full-screen mode** to make sure it works. Tap the **green flag** to start. Try out the **wrong answers** as well as the right answer.

You could **test** your quiz on a friend or family member.

Try this challenge, then tick the box when you've completed it.

I can plan, create and code my own animal quiz.

Fitness instructor

Time for some exercise! This talking fitness app will guide you through an exercise routine.

1️⃣ Choose a **new project**, the gym **background** and a **character** to be the fitness instructor.

2️⃣ Think of three different **exercises** to include in your routine, like star jumps or squats. **Write** or **draw** them in the boxes below.

Exercise 1	Exercise 2	Exercise 3

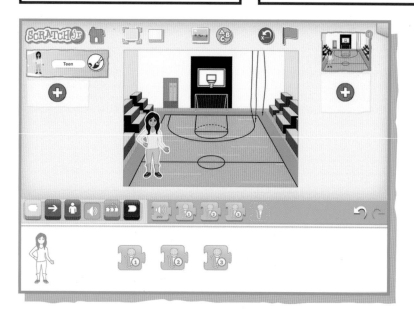

3️⃣ **Record** the fitness instructor calling out each of your **exercises**. Why not try out some funny voices!

You can have a maximum of five recordings for each character.

(4) Begin coding your instructor with a **start on tap** block or a **green flag**, then work out the order of your **exercises**.

Plan the order of your code here

Don't forget you can use each recorded instruction more than once.

Wait block code

Change the length of time to **wait** by tapping on the down arrow and **typing** in a new number.

Repeat loop code

Change the number of times you want a section repeated by **typing** in a new number.

(5) You can add a **wait block** after the first **instruction** so you keep doing that exercise until you hear the pop **sound**.

(6) Try putting a **sound block** and **wait block** inside a **repeat loop** so it gives you longer to complete the exercise.

Circle what you would need to tap to stop your project if you used a repeat forever block.

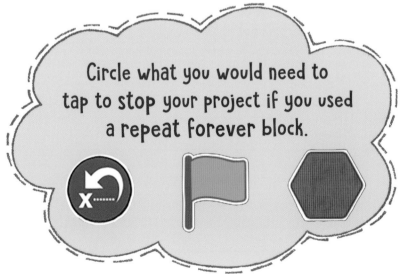

(7) Try out your **routine** and keep tweaking the **code blocks** until you're happy.

(8) Why not **record** a "Well done!" message to add to the end of your routine.

ANSWERS: The red hexagon stops a program from running

Well done!

27

Wake up alarm

Create a Voice Assistant app to wake up the kitten when it's time to get up!

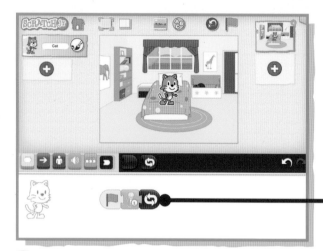

① Start a **new project** with the bedroom **background** and position the kitten on the bed.

② **Record** a snoring sound for the kitten, then add this **code** so it keeps snoring.

③ Add a **new character** and tap the **paintbrush** to edit it. Draw a long, black rectangle, then use the **fill tool** to fill it in. This is your Voice Assistant gadget.

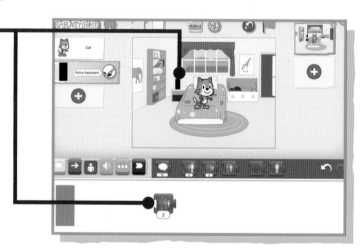

④ **Drag** the Voice Assistant to the bedside table. Add a **shrink block** to its coding area and tap it so it fits the table.

⑤ **Plan** your alarm sound/message here, then add the **code**.

Voice Assistant code

What annoying alarm could you **record** for the Voice Assistant? Write it here, then record it.

⑥ Create a **new character** and draw an eye mask shape for the kitten.

Don't take your pen off the paper at all!

Practise drawing an eye mask here. What colours and **patterns** will you choose?

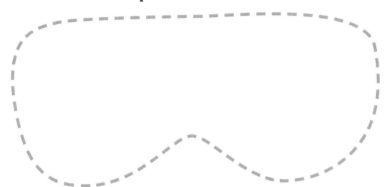

⑦ Drag the eye mask onto the kitten. Use the **shrink block** to make it fit.

⑧ Create another **sound block** for the kitten that says, "Alarm off."

⑨ Add these extra bits of **code** to your characters.

Extra kitten code

This extra code tells the kitten to: **stop** snoring when it's tapped, send a **message** to the eye mask, **play** the "alarm off" recording and finally send another **message** to the Voice Assistant.

Eye mask code

This code tells the eye mask to **hide** when it receives the **orange message**.

Extra Voice Assistant code

This extra code tells the Voice Assistant to **stop** the alarm when it receives the **red message**.

Don't forget to tap reset to start your program from the beginning.

⑩ Tap the **green flag** to start the kitten snoring, then tap the Voice Assistant and the kitten to run your program.

Well done!

Recording tips

Here are a few tips to help you make the most of your sound effects and voice recordings.

You can **record** five different **sound blocks** for each character.

> You can record sounds from the **real world** or use objects that create interesting sounds.

You can't **move** sounds between characters, but you can **send a message** to a character to play a sound.

Recordings of a character can be **copied** to another page if you **drag the character** to the new page. (All the character's code will be copied too, include the recording.)

> Shorter recordings are easier to make and use, but sometimes longer recordings are useful, especially if you're creating **music**.

If you **play an instrument** you can record yourself playing a tune.

Speak or **sing** clearly and don't shout!

> Check out the other books in this series to learn how to create more **characters** and turn your ideas into **animations** and **games**.